CW00649352

# how2become

# KS2 MATHS IS EASY

## (NUMBERS AND CALCULATIONS)

THE
**REVISION**
SERIES

**www.How2Become.com**

As part of this product you have also received FREE access to online tests that will help you to pass Key Stage 2 MATHS (Numbers and Calculations).

To gain access, simply go to:

# www.PsychometricTestsOnline.co.uk

Get more products
for passing any test at:

# www.how2become.com

Orders: Please contact How2become Ltd, Suite 2, 50 Churchill Square Business Centre, Kings Hill, Kent ME19 4YU.

You can order through Amazon.co.uk under ISBN 978-1-910602-47-8, via the website www.How2Become.com or through Gardners.com.

ISBN: 978-1-910602-47-8

First published in 2015 by How2become Ltd.

Copyright © 2015 How2become. All rights reserved.

All rights reserved. Apart from any permitted use under UK copyright law, no part of this publication may be reproduced or transmitted in any form or by any means, electronic or mechanical, including photocopying, recording, or any information, storage or retrieval system, without permission in writing from the publisher or under licence from the Copyright Licensing Agency Limited. Further details of such licenses (for reprographic reproduction) may be obtained from the Copyright Licensing Agency Ltd, Saffron House, 6-10 Kirby Street, London EC1N 8TS.

Typeset for How2become Ltd by Anton Pshinka.

## Disclaimer

Every effort has been made to ensure that the information contained within this guide is accurate at the time of publication. How2become Ltd are not responsible for anyone failing any part of any selection process as a result of the information contained within this guide. How2become Ltd and their authors cannot accept any responsibility for any errors or omissions within this guide, however caused. No responsibility for loss or damage occasioned by any person acting, or refraining from action, as a result of the material in this publication can be accepted by How2become Ltd.

The information within this guide does not represent the views of any third party service or organisation.

# CONTENTS

THE
**REVISION**
SERIES

# NUMBERS
# AND
# PLACE VALUES

## NUMBERS AND PLACE VALUES

### UNDERSTANDING NUMBERS AND DIGITS

Numbers are made up of **digits**.

1  2  3  4  5  6  7  8  9  0

You can put digits together in order to make bigger numbers.

*Example*

25 is made up of the digits 2 and 5

678 is made up of the digits 6, 7 and 8

### ODD AND EVEN NUMBERS

Numbers are either **odd** or **even**.

**Odd numbers** end in the following = 1, 3, 5, 7 or 9
**Even numbers** end in the following = 2, 4, 6, 8 or 0

You can work out whether big numbers are odd or even based on the last digit of the number.

**42,246** is an even number because it ends in a '6', and '6' is an even number.

**12,821** is an odd number because it ends in a '1', and '1' is an odd number.

### WHOLE NUMBERS AND DECIMALS

Whole numbers are any numbers that don't have a remainder (i.e. 47, 5, 948 and so forth). Decimals include a whole number and smaller parts of a number (i.e. 10.25 is 10 whole units plus .25).

10 is a whole number.

10.1 is a decimal number. It is bigger than 10, because it has 10 whole bits plus .1.

## NUMBERS AND PLACE VALUES

## PLACE VALUE HEADINGS

Below, we have demonstrated the most common place value headings that you will be expected to learn.

| Millions | Hundred Thousands | Ten Thousands | Thousands | Hundreds | Tens | Units | DECIMAL POINT | Tenths | Hundredths |
|---|---|---|---|---|---|---|---|---|---|
| | | | | | | | | | |

### Example 1

| Millions | Hundred Thousands | Ten Thousands | Thousands | Hundreds | Tens | Units | DECIMAL POINT | Tenths | Hundredths |
|---|---|---|---|---|---|---|---|---|---|
| | | | | 3 | 7 | 9 | • | | |

This number represents **379**

- The **3** represents **3 hundred;**
- The **7** represents **7 tens** or **seventy;**
- The **9** represents **9 units.**

### Example 2

| Millions | Hundred Thousands | Ten Thousands | Thousands | Hundreds | Tens | Units | DECIMAL POINT | Tenths | Hundredths |
|---|---|---|---|---|---|---|---|---|---|
| 3 | 2 | 4 | 6 | 1 | 7 | 9 | • | | |

This number represents **3,246,179**

- The **3** represents **3 million;**
- The **2, 4** and **6** represents **246 thousand;**
- The **1** represents **1 hundred;**
- The **7** represents **7 tens** or **seventy;**
- The **9** represents **9 units.**

### Now you try!

Write **72,356,210.3** in the correct place value headings.

| Millions | Hundred Thousands | Ten Thousands | Thousands | Hundreds | Tens | Units | DECIMAL POINT | Tenths | Hundredths |
|---|---|---|---|---|---|---|---|---|---|
| 72 | 3 | 5 | 6 | 2 | 1 | 0 | • | 3 | |

## NUMBERS AND PLACE VALUES

## WRITING NUMBERS IN WORDS

If you understand the value of each digit in a number, it should be fairly easy for you to write out the number in words.

*Example 1*

What is **509** in words?

**Step 1** = let's use our place value headings to break up the number.

| Hundreds | Tens | Units |
|:---:|:---:|:---:|
| 5 | 0 | 9 |

**Step 2** = to write out three-digit numbers, you should write the hundreds, then "and", followed by the tens and units.

**Step 3** = so **509** can be written as:

**Five hundred and nine**

**NOTE** = *there are no tens, so you would just say 'and 9'.*

Example 2

What is **24,312** in words?

**Step 1** = begin by writing the number out using place value headings.

| Ten Thousands | Thousands | Hundreds | Tens | Units |
|:---:|:---:|:---:|:---:|:---:|
| 2 | 4 | 3 | 1 | 2 |

**Step 2** = the **2** and **4** represents **24 thousand**;
the **3** represents **3 hundred**;
the **1** represents **1 ten** or **ten**;
the **2** represents **2 units**.

**Step 3** = so **24,312** can be written as:

**Twenty-four thousand three hundred and twelve**

## NUMBERS AND PLACE VALUES

## UNDERSTANDING BIG NUMBERS

In order to break up big numbers, you should remember the following method:

$$6257943.$$

**Step 1** = from the right (where the bullet point would be), make a space between **every 3 digits**.

$$6\ 257\ 943.$$

**Step 2** = this helps you to see what the digits are representing. You should treat these numbers as separate numbers.

**Step 3** = so 6, represents 6 million;
257 represents the thousands;
943 represents the hundreds.

**Step 4** = so the number in words is:

**Six million two hundred and fifty-seven thousand nine hundred and forty-three.**

*Now you try!*

Write 347,215 in words.

## Question 1

Write **79** in words.

## Question 2

Write **413** in words.

## Question 3

Write **92,375** in words.

## Question 4

Write **12,358,212** in words.

# Question 5

Using the place value headings below, write the following number in the correct columns:

**42,312.5**

| Millions | Hundred Thousands | Ten Thousands | Thousands | Hundreds | Tens | Units | DECIMAL POINT | Tenths | Hundredths |
|---|---|---|---|---|---|---|---|---|---|
| | | 4 | 2 | 3 | 1 | 2 | • | 5 | |

# Question 6

Using the place value headings below, write the following number in the correct columns:

**1,036,310.12**

| Millions | Hundred Thousands | Ten Thousands | Thousands | Hundreds | Tens | Units | DECIMAL POINT | Tenths | Hundredths |
|---|---|---|---|---|---|---|---|---|---|
| 1 | 0 | 3 | 6 | 3 | 1 | 0 | • | 1 | 2 |

# Question 7

Using the place value headings below, write the following number in the correct columns:

**413,579**

| Millions | Hundred Thousands | Ten Thousands | Thousands | Hundreds | Tens | Units | DECIMAL POINT | Tenths | Hundredths |
|---|---|---|---|---|---|---|---|---|---|
| | 4 | 1 | 3 | 5 | 7 | 9 | • | | |

# Question 8

Using the place value headings below, write the following number in the correct columns:

**90,205,104**

| Millions | Hundred Thousands | Ten Thousands | Thousands | Hundreds | Tens | Units | DECIMAL POINT | Tenths | Hundredths |
|---|---|---|---|---|---|---|---|---|---|
| 90 | 2 | 0 | 5 | 1 | 0 | 4 | • | | |

# ANSWERS TO NUMBERS AND PLACE VALUES

**Q1. Your answer should read as follows:**

*'Seventy-nine'*

**Q2. Your answer should read as follows:**

*'Four hundred and thirteen'*

**Q3. Your answer should read as follows:**

*'Ninety-two thousand three hundred and seventy-five'*

**Q4. Your answer should read as follows:**

*'Twelve million three hundred and fifty-eight thousand two hundred and twelve'*

**Q5. Your answer should look like this:**

| Millions | Hundred Thousands | Ten Thousands | Thousands | Hundreds | Tens | Units | DECIMAL POINT | Tenths | Hundredths |
|---|---|---|---|---|---|---|---|---|---|
|  |  | 4 | 2 | 3 | 1 | 2 | • | 5 |  |

**Q6. Your answer should look like this:**

| Millions | Hundred Thousands | Ten Thousands | Thousands | Hundreds | Tens | Units | DECIMAL POINT | Tenths | Hundredths |
|---|---|---|---|---|---|---|---|---|---|
| 1 | 0 | 3 | 6 | 3 | 1 | 0 | • | 1 | 2 |

**Q7. Your answer should look like this:**

| Millions | Hundred Thousands | Ten Thousands | Thousands | Hundreds | Tens | Units | DECIMAL POINT | Tenths | Hundredths |
|---|---|---|---|---|---|---|---|---|---|
|  | 4 | 1 | 3 | 5 | 7 | 9 | • |  |  |

**Q8. Your answer should look like this:**

| Millions | Hundred Thousands | Ten Thousands | Thousands | Hundreds | Tens | Units | DECIMAL POINT | Tenths | Hundredths |
|---|---|---|---|---|---|---|---|---|---|
| 90 | 2 | 0 | 5 | 1 | 0 | 4 | • |  |  |

**HOW ARE YOU GETTING ON?**

# ESTIMATING YOUR ANSWERS

## ESTIMATING YOUR ANSWERS

## ESTIMATE YOUR ANSWERS BY ROUNDING

If you are given a sum, you can roughly work out what your answer is going to be by rounding the numbers up or down, to make the sum easier to understand.

*Example 1*

Work out 387 + 206

Let's estimate the answer.

**Step 1** = 387 is almost 400
**Step 2** = 206 is almost 200
**Step 3** = so 400 + 200 = 600
**Step 4** = so you know your answer is going to be close enough to 600. This will ensure that when you come to calculate the ACTUAL answer, you have a guide as to what the answer will be.
**Step 5** = the actual answer would be = 387 + 206 = 593
**Step 6** =as you can see, your estimation was fairly close to the actual answer.

## ESTIMATING YOUR ANSWERS

Estimate the following by rounding the numbers up or down:

**Q1.** 87 + 63          160

**Q2.** 103 – 71         30

**Q3.** 329 + 349        6 50

**Q4.** 532 + 184

**Q5.** 2942 – 230

**Q6.** 396 – 49

**Q7.** 1003 + 2787

**Q8.** 5903 – 1579

(Remember, these are just estimations, not the ACTUAL answers!)

**Q1.** 50, **Q2.** 30, **Q3.** 600, **Q4.** 700, **Q5.** 2,800, **Q6.** 350, **Q7.** 3800, **Q8.** 4000

Answers

THE
**REVISION**
SERIES

# ROUNDING NUMBERS UP AND DOWN

## ROUNDING NUMBERS UP AND DOWN

### DIFFERENT WAYS TO ROUND UP A NUMBER

You may be asked to round a number up or down. There are several ways in which this question might be asked to you:

| To the nearest **ten** (10) | To the nearest **hundred** (100) | To the nearest **thousand** (1,000) |
| --- | --- | --- |
| To the nearest **ten thousand** (10,000) | To the nearest **hundred thousand** (100,000) | To the nearest **million** (1,000,000) |
| | To the nearest **whole number** | |

- To work out how to round off the number is relatively easy if you remember TWO IMPORTANT THINGS!

    **TIP 1!**

    The number you are trying to round off is in between two possible choices.

    e.g. 56 is in between 50 and 60.

    The KEY is to work out what the number is CLOSEST to.

    e.g. so 56 is closer to 60.

    **TIP 2!**

    If the number is in the middle of two numbers, then you ALWAYS round UP!

    e.g. 55 is in between 50 and 60. Because it is in the middle of both these numbers, you would always round up!

## ROUNDING NUMBERS UP AND DOWN

## ROUNDING TO THE NEAREST 10

**To round to the nearest 10** = focus on the last digit

_REMEMBER_

If the unit (i.e. the last digit) is between 1 and 4 = **round down!**

If the unit (i.e. the last digit) is between 5 and 9 = **round up!**

_Example 1_

Round **213** to the nearest ten.

**Step 1** = look at the last digit = '3'.
**Step 2** = work out whether the last digit is between 1 and 4, or 5 and 9.
**Step 3** = you should know to round the number down because '3' is between 1 and 4.
**Step 4** = so, 213 to the nearest ten = 210.

_Example 2_

Round **2,575** to the nearest ten.

**Step 1** = look at the last digit = '5'.
**Step 2** = remember, 5 or more means you round up.
**Step 3** = so 2,575 to the nearest ten is 2,580.

_Now you try!_

Round **4,328** to the nearest ten.

## ROUNDING NUMBERS UP AND DOWN

### ROUNDING TO THE NEAREST 100

**To round to the nearest 100** = focus on the **tens** digit

_REMEMBER_

If the digit is between 1 and 4 = **round down!**

If the digit is between 5 and 9 = **round up!**

_Example 1_

Round **3,982** to the nearest hundred.

**Step 1** = look at the tens digit = '8'.
**Step 2** = work out whether the digit is between 1 and 4, or 5 and 9.
**Step 3** = you should know to round the number up because '8' is between 5 and 9.
**Step 4** = so, 3,982 to the nearest hundred = 4,000.

**NOTE:** because you rounded the 8 up, the number will change to 4,000. (982 is close to 1,000).

_Example 2_

Round **5,025** to the nearest hundred.

**Step 1** = look at the tens digit = '2'.
**Step 2** = remember, 4 or less means you round down.
**Step 3** = so 5,025 to the nearest hundred is 5,000.

_Now you try!_

Round **7,338** to the nearest hundred.

## ROUNDING NUMBERS UP AND DOWN

# ROUNDING TO THE NEAREST 1000

**To round to the nearest 1000** = focus on the **hundreds** digit
_REMEMBER_

If the digit is between 1 and 4 = **round down!**

If the digit is between 5 and 9 = **round up!**

_Example 1_

Round **3,449** to the nearest thousand.

**Step 1** = look at the hundreds digit = '4'.
**Step 2** = work out whether the last digit is between 1 and 4, or 5 and 9.
**Step 3** = you should know to round the number down because '4' is between 1 and 4.
**Step 4** = so, 3,449 to the nearest thousand = 3,000

_Example 2_

Round **7,623** to the nearest thousand.

**Step 1** = look at the hundreds digit = '6'
**Step 2** = remember, 5 or more means you round up.
**Step 3** = so 7,623 to the nearest thousand is 8,000.

# ROUNDING UP TO THE NEAREST WHOLE NUMBER

This is very easy. You just need to find which whole number is closest to the number you are working out.

_Example 1_

43.26 to the nearest whole number

**Step 1** = the .26 is less than half of a whole number. Therefore you would round down.
**Step 2** = so 43.26 to the nearest whole number = 43.

## ROUNDING NUMBERS UP AND DOWN

### ROUNDING TO DECIMAL PLACES

**Step 1** = work out the position of the digit you are rounding to.
**Step 2** = then look at the next number, which will be the decider.
**Step 3** = if the decider number is 5 or more, you will round up. If the number is less than 5, you will round down.

You are more than likely going to be given questions that ask you to round off to a certain number of decimal places.

*Example 1*

What is 42.45 rounded to 1 decimal place?

- You are rounding to 1 decimal place, so you will focus on the first number after the decimal point (4).
- The decider number is (5). This means that you will round up.
- So 42.45 to 1 decimal place is **42.5**

*Example 2*

What is 314.326 rounded to 2 decimal places?

- For this question you are rounding to 2 decimal places, which means two numbers will need to remain in the answer.
- The '6' is the decider. This means you need to round up!
- So 314.326 to 2 decimal places is **314.33**

*Now you try!*

What is **45.64** to 1 decimal place?     What is **312.4562** to 2 decimal places?

## Question 1

Round the following number to the nearest **ten**.

**23**

## Question 2

Round the following number to the nearest **ten**.

**89**

## Question 3

Round the following number to the nearest **hundred**.

**237**

## Question 4

Round the following number to the nearest **hundred**.

**575**

## Question 5

Round the following number to the nearest **thousand**.

**3,432**

## Question 6

Anil needs your help. He thinks if he rounds the number 457 to the nearest hundred, it will round down.

Is Anil correct? Please circle your answer and explain your reasons.

# Yes/No

_____

_____

_____

_____

## Question 7

Round the following number to the nearest whole number:

# 3.18

## Question 8

Round the following number to the nearest whole number:

# 24.56

## Question 9

Round the following number to 1 decimal place.

# 136.08

## Question 10

Anil needs your help. Below there are six numbers. Draw a line from the number 70 to all of the numbers that can be rounded to 70, if they were to be rounded to the nearest 10.

70

65    68    61        63    69    64

## Question 11

What is the following number rounded to the nearest:

3,027,456

a) Ten

b) Hundred

c) Thousand

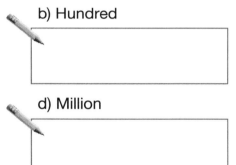

d) Million

## Question 12

I think of a prime number between 10 and 20. I double it. Rounded to the nearest ten, the number is 20. What number did I start with?

## ANSWERS TO ROUNDING UP AND DOWN

### Q1. 20

EXPLANATION = 23 to the nearest 10 = 20. ('3' is less than 5, so we round down).

### Q2. 90

EXPLANATION = 89 to the nearest 10 = 90. ('9' is more than 5, so we round up).

### Q3. 200

EXPLANATION = 237 to the nearest 100 = 200. ('3' is less than 5, so we round down).

### Q4. 600

EXPLANATION = 575 to the nearest 100 = 600. ('7' is more than 5, so we round up).

### Q5. 3,000

EXPLANATION = 3,432 to the nearest thousand = 3,000. ('4' is less than 5 so we round down).

### Q6. No

EXPLANATION = Anil is not correct in his assumption. If you rounded 457 to the nearest 100, you would have to round up. The '5' in the middle means you would round up. So 457 is closer to 500.

### Q7. 3

EXPLANATION = 3.18 to the nearest whole number = 3. The number 3.18 is in between 3 and 4, and it is closer to 3.

### Q8. 25

EXPLANATION = 24.56 to the nearest whole number = 25. The number 24.56 is in between 24 and 25, and it is closer to 25.

**Q9. 136.1**

EXPLANATION = 136.08 to the nearest 1 decimal place = 136.1. The decider number '8' is higher than 5, so you would round up.

**Q10. Your answer should look something like this:**

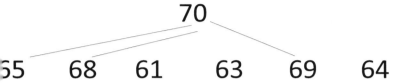

55    68    61    63    69    64

**Q11. a) 3,027,460**

EXPLANATION = 3,027,456 to the nearest 10 would be 3,027,460. The '56' is closer to '60'.

**b) 3,027,500**

EXPLANATION = 3,027,456 to the nearest 100 would be 3,027,500. The '456' is closer to '500'.

**c) 3,027,000**

EXPLANATION = 3,027,456 to the nearest 1000 would be 3,027,000. The '7,456' is closer to '7,000' than '8,000'.

**d) 3,000,000**

EXPLANATION = 3,027,456 to the nearest million is 3,000,000. The '0' means that it is closer to 3 million as opposed to 4 million.

**Q12. 11**

EXPLANATION = I think of a prime number between 10 and 20 (11). I double it (22). Rounded to the nearest 10, this would be 20.

**HOW ARE YOU GETTING ON?**

THE
**REVISION**
SERIES

# NEGATIVE AND POSITIVE NUMBERS

## NEGATIVE AND POSITIVE NUMBERS

## NEGATIVE AND POSITIVE NUMBERS

Positive Numbers  any number ABOVE '0'.

Negative Numbers  any number BELOW '0'.

The best way to understand positive and negative numbers is to use a number line.

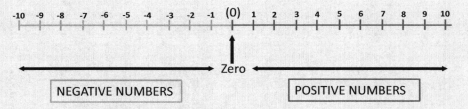

| NEGATIVE NUMBERS | | POSITIVE NUMBERS |

Negative numbers are another word for 'minus'.

Negative numbers are often used to refer to really cold temperatures. The higher the number, the colder it is.

Positive numbers are another word for 'plus'.

Positive numbers are often used to refer to warm temperatures. The higher the number, the hotter it is.

If you move from zero to the right, the further you go, the bigger the number.

If you move from zero to the left, the further you go, the lower the number.

**NOTE:** a lot of people make the mistake that -10 is higher than -7 because the number is bigger, these people are wrong!

-10 is further down the number line which means the number is further away from zero, and is therefore smaller.

## NEGATIVE AND POSITIVE NUMBERS

## ADDING AND SUBTRACTING NEGATIVE NUMBERS

If you are adding negative numbers ⟹ count towards the **right**.

If you are subtracting negative numbers ⟹ count towards the **left**.

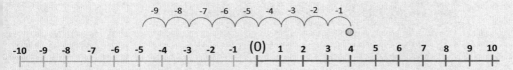

What is 4 − 9?

**Step 1** = find '4' on the number line. Remember if there is no sign before a number, it is positive (+).

**Step 2** = you are subtracting, which means you need to count backwards i.e. to the left.

**Step 3** = after counting back 9, you should end up on -5. This is the answer.

## _Now you try!_

What is 6 − 12?

What is 0 − 9?

What is -5 + 7?

What is -9 + 11?

What is -1 − 6?

What is 4 − 10?

## NEGATIVE AND POSITIVE NUMBERS

### UNDERSTANDING SIGNS

If two signs appear next to one another, you need to know what to do.

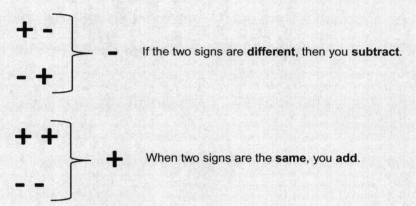

**+ -**

**- +**

**-** If the two signs are **different**, then you **subtract**.

**+ +**

**- -**

**+** When two signs are the **same**, you **add**.

*Example*

20 + -6 (a '+' and a '-' equals a minus). So 20 – 6 = 14.

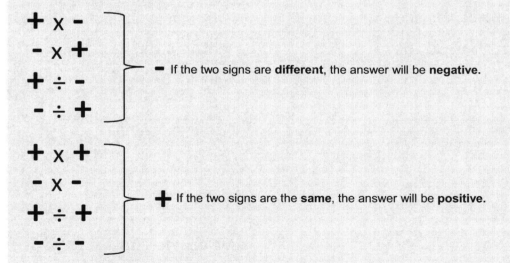

**+ x -**

**- x +**

**+ ÷ -**

**- ÷ +**

**-** If the two signs are **different**, the answer will be **negative**.

**+ x +**

**- x -**

**+ ÷ +**

**- ÷ -**

**+** If the two signs are the **same**, the answer will be **positive**.

*Example*

-12 x -2 (there are two minus numbers which means the answer will be positive). So, 12 x 2 = 24

## Question 1

Using the number line to help, what is 10 + -4?

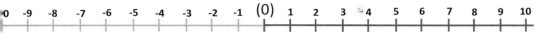

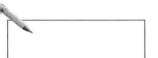

## Question 2

Using the number line to help, what is 5 - -3?

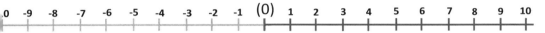

## Question 3

Using the number line to help, what is -8 x 6?

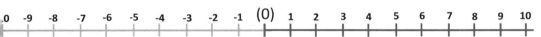

## Question 4

Using the number line to help, what is -9 ÷ 3?

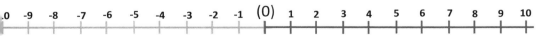

## Question 5

Arrange these numbers from coldest to hottest.

**4°C    -6°C    17°C    -10°C    0°C    2°C    -3°C**

## Question 6

Study the following table below and answer the following questions.

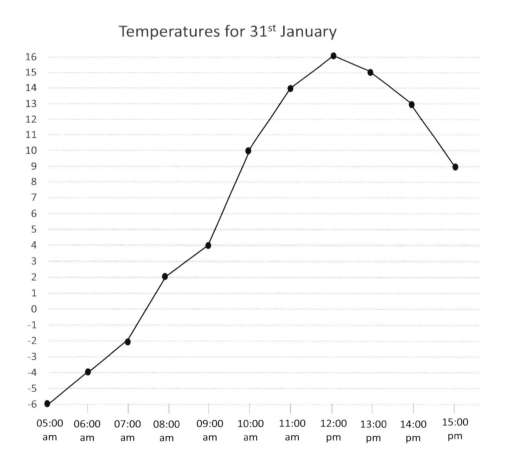

Temperatures for 31ˢᵗ January

a) What was the temperature at 05:00am?

b) What was the difference in temperature between 08:00am and 09:00am?

c) On how many occasions on the 31st January was the temperature below freezing?

d) If the temperature continued to drop 2°C every hour from 3 o'clock onwards, what would the approximate temperature be at 19:00pm?

e) What was the approximate temperature at 13:30pm?

## Question 7

Below are six numbers. Using the high to low chart, write the numbers in the correct order.

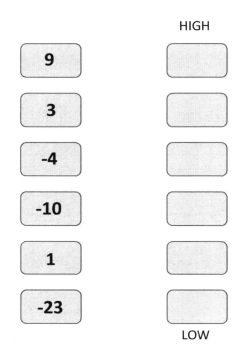

HIGH

9

3

-4

-10

1

-23

LOW

# ANSWERS TO NEGATIVE AND POSITIVE NUMBERS

**Q1. 6**

EXPLANATION = 10 + -4 (+ - equals a minus). So
10 – 4 = 6.

**Q2. 8**

EXPLANATION = 5 - -3 (- - equals a plus). So 5 + 3 = 8

**Q3. -48**

EXPLANATION = -8 x 6 (- X + equals negative). So -8 x 6 = -48

**Q4. -3**

EXPLANATION = -9 ÷ 3 (- ÷ + equals negative). So -9 ÷ 3 = -3

**Q5. -10°C, -6°C, -3°C, 0°C, 2°C, 4°C, 17°C**

EXPLANATION = coldest (will be negative numbers). Remember, -10°C is
colder than -6°C.

**Q6. a) -6°C**

EXPLANATION = the temperature at 05:00am is -6°C.

**b) 2°C**

EXPLANATION = the difference in temperature between 08:00 and 09:00 is
2°C. At 08:00 it was 2°C, and at 09:00 it was 4°C.

**c) 3**

EXPLANATION = three occasions saw the temperature below freezing (05:00
= -6°C, 06:00 = -4°C, 07:00 = -2°C).

**d) 1°C**

EXPLANATION = if the temperature were to drop 2°C every hour from 3
o'clock onwards. So at 3 o'clock, the temperature was 9°C. There are 4 hours
from then until 7 o'clock. So 4 x 2 (4 hours, dropping 2°C every 2 hours) = 8.
So, 9°C - 8°C = 1°C.

e) **14°C**

EXPLANATION = the temperature at 13:30 is 14°C.

**Q7. Your answer should look something like this:**

HIGH

| -23 | 9 |
|---|---|
| 3 | 3 |
| -4 | 1 |
| -10 | -4 |
| 9 | -10 |
| 1 | -23 |

LOW

**HOW ARE YOU GETTING ON?**

THE
**REVISION**
SERIES

# ROMAN NUMERALS

## ROMAN NUMERALS

## WHAT ARE ROMAN NUMERALS?

Roman numerals were established by the Ancient Romans. They used letters to represent numbers.

Below is a list of the common Roman numerals you are expected to know.

| | | | |
|---|---|---|---|
| **1 = I** | **2 = II** | **3 = III** | **4 = IV** |
| **5 = V** | **6 = VI** | **7 = VII** | **8 = VIII** |
| **9 = IX** | **10 = X** | **20 = XX** | **30 = XXX** |
| **40 = XL** | **50 = L** | **60 = LX** | **70 = LXX** |
| **80 = LXXX** | **90 = XC** | **100 = C** | **500 = D** |
| **1,000 = M** | | | |

> The Romans didn't have a number for zero!

## HOW TO WRITE A NUMBER IN ROMAN NUMERALS

**Step 1** = you should focus on these Roman numerals.
**Step 2** = all of these Roman numerals can be used to form ANY number.

| | | | |
|---|---|---|---|
| **1 = I** | **5 = V** | **10 = X** | **50 = L** |
| **100 = C** | **500 = D** | **1,000 = M** | |

*Example*

How to write **8** in Roman numerals

**Step 1** = Roman numerals are made by adding or subtracting numbers.

**Step 2** = using the above Roman numerals, you would use 5 + 1 + 1 + 1.

**Step 3** = change the numbers into their Roman numeral symbol = V + I + I + I.

# REMEMBER = write the BIGGEST number first!

## Question 1

Using the below numbers, write the equivalent Roman numeral. The first one has been done for you.

| 21 | XXI | 32 | ———— |
|:---:|:---:|:---:|:---:|
| 43 | ———— | 54 | ———— |
| 65 | ———— | 76 | ———— |
| 87 | ———— | 98 | ———— |
| 119 | ———— | 135 | ———— |

## Question 2

Match the Roman numerals with the correct number. The first one has been done for you.

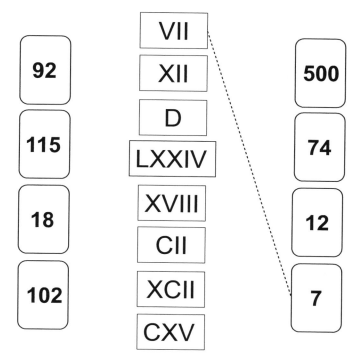

92   115   18   102

VII   XII   D   LXXIV   XVIII   CII   XCII   CXV

500   74   12   7

## Question 3

Anil needs your help. For the following sentences, he needs to work out what the Roman numerals are representing in order to work out the calculations. Read the sentences and then write your answers (in numbers) in the space provided.

a) Anil spent £L in V days. What is the average amount of money he spent per day?

b) Anil has XLII superhero costumes. How many costumes does Anil have?

c) Anil's best friend Scarlett loves pearls. Anil gives Scarlett a necklace which contains XLVI. Anil also gives her a pearl bracelet that contains XVIII pearls. How many pearls does Anil give Scarlett?

## Question 4

Work out what time it is using the Roman numeral clocks.

a)

b)

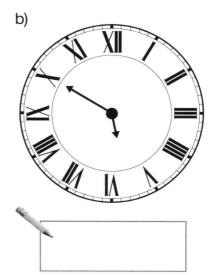

# ANSWERS TO ROMAN NUMERALS

**Q1. Your answer should look something like this:**

| | | | |
|---|---|---|---|
| 21 | *XXI* | 32 | XXXII |
| 43 | XLIII | 54 | LIV |
| 65 | LXV | 76 | LXXVI |
| 87 | LXXXVII | 98 | XCVIII |
| 119 | CXIX | 135 | CXXXV |

**Q2. Your answer should look something like this:**

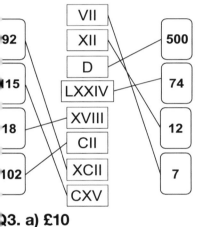

**Q3. a) £10**

EXPLANATION = 'L' = 50. 'V' = 5. So, £50 ÷ 5 = £10 per day.

    **b) 42**

EXPLANATION = 'XLII' = 42.

    **c) 64**

EXPLANATION = 'XLVI' = 46. 'XVIII' = 18. So, 46 + 18 = 64.

**Q4. a) 4:10**

    **b) 5:50**

**HOW ARE YOU GETTING ON?**

THE
**REVISION**
SERIES

# SQUARE, CUBE, TRIANGLE AND PRIME NUMBERS

## SQUARE, CUBE, TRIANGLE AND PRIME NUMBERS

### WHAT ARE SQUARE NUMBERS?

Square numbers are really easy!

It is a number that is multiplied by **itself**!

The symbol that represents a 'squared' number is '$^2$'.

$$1^2 = 1 \times 1 = 1 \qquad 6^2 = 6 \times 6 = 36$$
$$2^2 = 2 \times 2 = 2 \qquad 7^2 = 7 \times 7 = 49$$
$$3^2 = 3 \times 3 = 9 \qquad 8^2 = 8 \times 8 = 64$$
$$4^2 = 4 \times 4 = 16 \qquad 9^2 = 9 \times 9 = 81$$
$$5^2 = 5 \times 5 = 25 \qquad 10^2 = 10 \times 10 = 100$$

*Let's break this down even further, and use ACTUAL squares to visualise the squared numbers.*

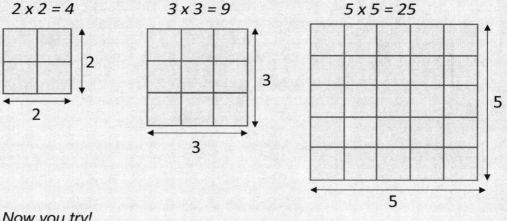

*2 x 2 = 4*    *3 x 3 = 9*    *5 x 5 = 25*

<u>*Now you try!*</u>

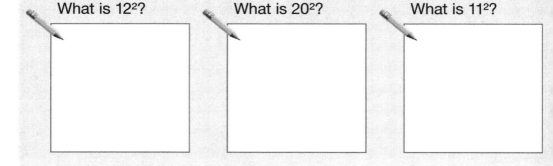

What is 12$^2$?    What is 20$^2$?    What is 11$^2$?

## SQUARE, CUBE, TRIANGLE AND PRIME NUMBERS

## SQUARE ROOTS

The square root of a number is a number that can be multiplied by itself, in order to give you the squared number.

As shown above, the squared numbers from 1-100 are as follows:

**1    2    9    16    (25)    36    49    64    81    100**

- So, these are the squared numbers.
- To work out the square root of these numbers, you need to work out what number was multiplied in order to reach this number.

*Let's use **25** as our example*

What is the square root of 25?

**Step 1** = what number can be multiplied by itself in order to make 25?
**Step 2** = you should know that the square root of 25 is 5. (5 x 5 = 25).

## SQUARE ROOT SYMBOL

The symbol used for square root is:

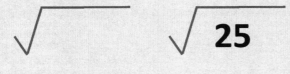

*Now you try!*

What is the square root of 81?

What is the square root of 121?

## SQUARE, CUBE, TRIANGLE AND PRIME NUMBERS

### WHAT ARE CUBED NUMBERS?

Cubed numbers are simple if you have already mastered squared numbers!

It is a number that is multiplied by **itself THREE times**!

The symbol that represents a 'cubed' number is '$^3$'.

$$1^3 = 1 \times 1 \times 1 = 1$$
$$2^3 = 2 \times 2 \times 2 = 8$$
$$3^3 = 3 \times 3 \times 3 = 27$$
$$4^3 = 4 \times 4 \times 4 = 64$$
$$5^3 = 5 \times 5 \times 5 = 125$$

$$6^3 = 6 \times 6 \times 6 = 216$$
$$7^3 = 7 \times 7 \times 7 = 343$$
$$8^3 = 8 \times 8 \times 8 = 512$$
$$9^3 = 9 \times 9 \times 9 = 729$$
$$10^3 = 10 \times 10 \times 10 = 1,000$$

*Let's break this down even further, and use ACTUAL squares to visualise the squared numbers.*

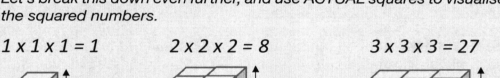

$1 \times 1 \times 1 = 1$      $2 \times 2 \times 2 = 8$      $3 \times 3 \times 3 = 27$

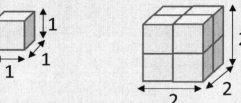

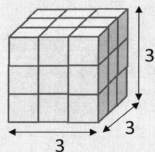

### WHAT ARE TRIANGLE NUMBERS?

Triangle numbers are numbers that make up a triangle. The best way to explain this is by example.

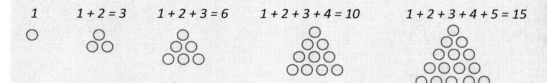

$1$      $1 + 2 = 3$      $1 + 2 + 3 = 6$      $1 + 2 + 3 + 4 = 10$      $1 + 2 + 3 + 4 + 5 = 15$

## SQUARE, CUBE, TRIANGLE AND PRIME NUMBERS

# WHAT ARE PRIME NUMBERS?

A prime number is a number than can only be divided by itself and 1.

*Below I have written out the prime numbers from 1 – 100.*

| 1 | 2 | 3 | 4 | 5 | 6 | 7 | 8 | 9 | 10 |
|---|---|---|---|---|---|---|---|---|---|
| 11 | 12 | 13 | 14 | 15 | 16 | 17 | 18 | 19 | 20 |
| 21 | 22 | 23 | 24 | 25 | 26 | 27 | 28 | 29 | 30 |
| 31 | 32 | 33 | 34 | 35 | 36 | 37 | 38 | 39 | 40 |
| 41 | 42 | 43 | 44 | 45 | 46 | 47 | 48 | 49 | 50 |
| 51 | 52 | 53 | 54 | 55 | 56 | 57 | 58 | 59 | 60 |
| 61 | 62 | 63 | 64 | 65 | 66 | 67 | 68 | 69 | 70 |
| 71 | 72 | 73 | 74 | 75 | 76 | 77 | 78 | 79 | 80 |
| 81 | 82 | 83 | 84 | 85 | 86 | 87 | 88 | 89 | 90 |
| 91 | 92 | 93 | 94 | 95 | 96 | 97 | 98 | 99 | 100 |

*Example 1*

**23** is a prime number because only the numbers 1 and 23 can be multiplied together in order to get 23. No other numbers can be divided equally into 23.

*Example 2*

**9** is **NOT** a prime number. The numbers 1, 9 and 3 can all be divided into 9.

If a number has more than 2 numbers that can be multiplied, then the number is NOT a prime number.

## Question 1

Anil needs your help. Complete the table below by filling in the missin[g] numbers. The first one has been done for you.

| $x$ | $x^2$ | $x^3$ |
|---|---|---|
| 4 | 16 | 64 |
| _____ | 9 | _____ |
| _____ | _____ | 8 |
| 10 | _____ | _____ |

## Question 2

Below is a list of numbers. Write these numbers in the correct circle[s] depending on what *type* of number they are.

**23   41   15   19   25   36   49   4**

Prime numbers    Odd numbers    Square numbers

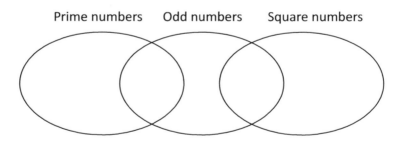

## Question 3

Work out the answers to the following questions.

a) $8^2$ _____        b) $4^3$_____

c) $11^2$ _____        d) $5^3$_____

## Question 4

Complete the following sequences below.

**1   3   6   10   15   21   28   ____   ____   55**

Using the above sequence, what *type* of numbers are these. Please circle the correct answer.

| Squared numbers | Cubed numbers | Triangular numbers | Prime numbers |

**31   37   ____   ____   47   53   ____   61   67   71   ____**

Using the above sequence, what *type* of numbers are these. Please circle the correct answer.

| Squared numbers | Cubed numbers | Triangular numbers | Prime numbers |

**1   4   9   ____   25   36   ____   ____   81   ____   ____**

Using the above sequence, what *type* of numbers are these. Please circle the correct answer.

| Squared numbers | Cubed numbers | Triangular numbers | Prime numbers |

## Question 5

Complete the following sums.

a) $3^2 + 5^2 = $ _____

b) $4^2 + 3^2 = $ _____

c) $5^2 - 2^2 = $ _____

d) $7^2 - 5^2 = $ _____

e) $4^2 \times 2^2 = $ _____

f) $4^2 \div 2^2 = $ _____

g) $3^3 + 2^3 = $ _____

h) $4^3 - 3^3 = $ _____

## Question 6

Fill in the missing blanks.

a)    Square          Square
      number          number

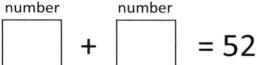

$= 52$

b)    Prime           Prime
      number          number

$= 60$

## Question 7

Anil thinks of a number between 1 and 30. The number he is thinking of is triangular number. List all of the possible numbers Anil could be thinking.

## ANSWERS TO SQUARE, CUBE, TRIANGLE AND PRIME NUMBERS

**1. Your answer should look like this:**

| X | $x^2$ | $x^3$ |
|---|---|---|
| 4 | 16 | 64 |
| 3 | 9 | 27 |
| 2 | 4 | 8 |
| 10 | 100 | 1,000 |

**2. Your answer should look something like this:**

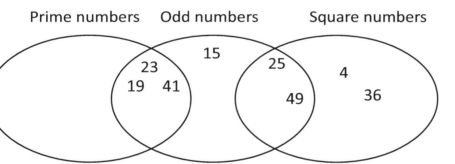

**3. a) 64**

EXPLANATION = 8 x 8 = 64

    **b) 64**

EXPLANATION = 4 x 4 = 16 x 4 = 64

    **c) 121**

EXPLANATION = 11 x 11 = 121

    **d) 125**

EXPLANATION = 5 x 5 = 25 x 5 = 125

**Q4. a) 36 and 45**

EXPLANATION = the difference between the increase of numbers increases by 1 each time (i.e. plus 2, plus 3, plus 4 etc…)

**b) Triangular numbers**

EXPLANATION = this is a triangular sequence.

**c) 41, 43, 59 and 73**

EXPLANATION = these are numbers that can only be divided by 1 and themselves.

**d) Prime numbers**

EXPLANATION = in sequence, these are prime numbers.

**e) 16, 49, 64, 100 and 121**

EXPLANATION = these numbers are square numbers.

**f) Square numbers**

EXPLANATION = these numbers are square numbers (numbers that are multiplied by themselves i.e. 5 x 5, 6 x 6 and so forth).

**Q5. a) 34**

EXPLANATION = $3^2 + 5^2 =$     3 x 3 = 9.       5 x 5 = 25.       9 + 25 = 34.

**b) 25**

EXPLANATION = $4^2 + 3^2 =$     4 x 4 = 16.       3 x 3 = 9.       16 + 9 = 25.

**c) 21**

EXPLANATION = $5^2 - 2^2 =$     5 x 5 = 25.       2 x 2 = 4.       25 − 4 = 21.

**d) 24**

EXPLANATION = $7^2 - 5^2 =$     7 x 7 = 49.       5 x 5 = 25.       49 − 25 = 24.

**e) 64**

EXPLANATION = $4^2 \times 2^2 =$     4 x 4 = 16.       2 x 2 = 4.       16 x 4 = 64.

**f) 4**

EXPLANATION = $4^2 \div 2^2 =$     4 x 4 = 16.       2 x 2 = 4.       16 ÷ 4 = 4.

**g) 35**

EXPLANATION = $3^3 + 2^3 =$    $3 \times 3 \times 3 = 27$.    $2 \times 2 \times 2 = 8$.    $27 + 8 = 35$.

**h) 37**

EXPLANATION = $4^3 - 3^3 =$    $4 \times 4 \times 4 = 64$.    $3 \times 3 \times 3 = 27$.    $64 - 27 = 37$.

**Q6. a) 36 and 16**

EXPLANATION = $36 + 16 = 52$

**b) 23 and 37**

EXPLANATION = $23 + 37 = 60$

*You could also have the combination of 31 + 29, 7 + 53, 13 + 47 and 19 + 41.*

**Q7. 1, 3, 6, 10, 15, 21, 28**

EXPLANATION = triangular numbers between 1 and 30 are listed above.
Therefore ALL of these numbers would have to be listed.

**HOW ARE YOU GETTING ON?**

# THE REVISION SERIES

# MULTIPLES AND FACTORS

## MULTIPLES AND FACTORS

### MULTIPLES

Multiples are just another word for times tables.

*Example 1*

The **multiples of 2**:

Remember, think of your 2 times tables.

- 2, 4, 6, 8, 10, 12, 14, 16, 18, 20 and so forth...

Note: multiples of 2 will always end in 2, 4, 6, 8 or 0. So 3,232 is a multiple of 2 because it ends in 2.

*Example 2*

The **multiples of 4**:

Remember, think of your 4 times tables.

- 4, 8, 12, 16, 20, 24, 28, 32, 36, 40 and so forth...

### FINDING THE LEAST COMMON MULTIPLE (LCM)

Finding the 'common' multiples of numbers means finding a number that they both have in common.

*Example 1*

Find the lowest common multiple of 2 and 5.

**Step 1** = write out the multiples of 2.
2, 4, 6, 8, 10,
**Step 2** = write out the multiples of 5.
5, 10, 15, 20, 25...
**Step 3** = find the lowest multiple that both 2 and 5 have in common.
**Step 4** = the lowest common multiple for 2 and 5 is 10. (There is no other smaller number that is a multiple of 2 and 5, therefore this is the correct answer).

## MULTIPLES AND FACTORS

# FACTORS

Factors are numbers that can be divided **EXACTLY** into other numbers.

Think of it this way:

Factors are just numbers that can be multiplied together to get another number.

What are all the factors of 12?

**Step 1** = this is basically asking you 'what numbers can be multiplied together to give you the answer of 12?'

**Step 2** = 1 x 12 = 12 (so both 1 and 12 are factors of 12)
       2 x 6 = 12 (so both 2 and 6 are factors of 12)
       3 x 4 = 12 (so both 3 and 4 are factors of 12).

**Step 3** = so in ascending order, the factors of 12 are:
       1, 2, 3, 4, 6 and 12

What are all the factors of 36?

**Step 1** = this is basically asking you 'what numbers can be multiplied together to give you the answer of 36?'

**Step 2** = 1 x 36 = 36 (so both 1 and 36 are factors of 36)
       2 x 18 = 36 (so both 2 and 18 are factors of 36)
       3 x 12 = 36 (so both 3 and 12 are factors of 36)
       4 x 9 = 36 (so both 4 and 9 are factors of 36)
       6 x 6 = 36 (so 6 is a factor of 36. Note you only count 6 once!)

**Step 3** = so in ascending order, the factors of 36 are:
       1, 2, 3, 4, 6, 9, 12, 18 and 36

PLEASE NOTE!

If a number only has the factors of 1 and itself, that means this number is prime (see the prime number chapter for further details).

_Example_

11 is a prime number because it only has the factors of 1 and 11 (1 x 11 = 11). No other numbers can be divided into 11.

## Question 1

What are the first twelve multiples of 6?

## Question 2

Place the following numbers in the correct part of the diagram.

**12  8  36  40  48  84  6  2**

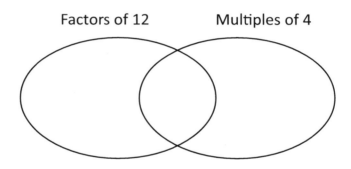

Factors of 12          Multiples of 4

## Question 3

a)  Write down ALL of the factors of 50.

b)  Write down ALL of the factors of 49.

## Question 4

ind the **lowest common multiple** for the following pairs of numbers.

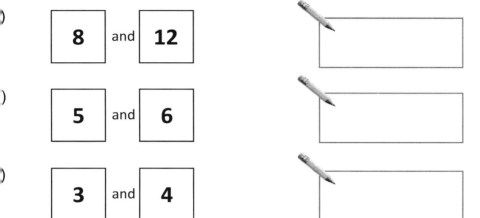

) 8 and 12

) 5 and 6

) 3 and 4

## Question 5

ind the **highest common factor** of 36 and 24.

## Question 6

ind the **highest common factor** of 25 and 20.

## Question 7

2 is a factor of 28. True of false. Please circle the correct answer.

**rue / False**

## Question 8
What is the **lowest common multiple** of 5, 6, and 9?

## Question 9
Write all of the multiples of 7, up to 100.

## Question 10
What is the **lowest common multiple** of 3, 5 and 30?

## Question 11
Explain the difference, using examples, between multiples and factors.

## Question 12
Write down the common factors of 54 and 72.

# ANSWERS TO MULTIPLES AND FACTORS

**Q1. 6, 12, 18, 24, 30, 36, 42, 48, 54, 60, 66 and 72**

EXPLANATION = remember, multiples are the times tables. So you need to write down the first twelve multiples in the 6 times table.

**Q2. Your answer should look something like this:**

**12   8   36   40   48   84   6   2**

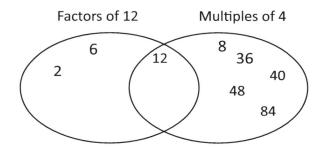

Factors of 12          Multiples of 4

6              8
12           36
2                    40
48
84

**Q3. a) 1 and 50, 2 and 25, 5 and 10**

EXPLANATION = remember factors are numbers that can be divided exactly into another number.

   **b) 1 and 49, 7**

EXPLANATION = remember factors are numbers that can be divided exactly into another number.

**Q4. a) 24**

EXPLANATION = Find the first few multiples of 8 = 8, 16, **24**...

          Find the first few multiples of 12 = 12, **24**, 36...

   **b) 30**

EXPLANATION = Find the first few multiples of 5 = 5, 10, 15, 20, 25, **30**...

          Find the first few multiples of 6 = 6, 12, 18, 24, **30**....

   **c) 12**

EXPLANATION = Find the first few multiples of 3 = 3, 6, 9, **12**...

          Find the first few multiples of 4 = 4, 8, **12**....

### Q5. 12

EXPLANATION = factors of 36 = 1, 2, 3, 4, 9, **12**, 18 and 36
Factors of 24 = 1, 2, 3, 4, 6, 8, **12**, and 24.

### Q6. 5

EXPLANATION = factors of 25 = 1, **5** and 25.
Factors of 20 = 1, 2, 4, **5** 10 and 20

### Q7. False

EXPLANATION = 12 is not a factor of 28. The factors of 28 are: 1, 2, 4, 7, 14 and 28.

### Q8. 90

EXPLANATION = multiples of 5 = (5 x 18).
Multiples of 6 = (6 x 15) Multiples of 9 (9 x 10)

### Q9. 7, 14, 21, 28, 35, 42, 49, 56, 63, 70, 77, 84, 91, 98

EXPLANATION = multiples of 7 is just the 7 times table.

### Q10. 30

EXPLANATION = the lowest common multiple will be 30. The number 30 will be the first number in this times table. Both 5 and 3 can be divided exactly into 30.

### Q11. Your answer should read something like this:

Multiples are simply times tables. For example, the multiples of 3 are 3, 6, 9, 12, 15 and so forth. Factors are numbers that can be divided into the number. For example the factors of 10 are 1 and 10 (1 x 10 = 10), and 2 and 5 (2 x 5).

### Q12. 1, 2, 3, 6, 9 and 18

EXPLANATION = factors of 54 are = 1, 2, 3, 6, 9, 18, 27 and 54.
The factors of 72 are = 1, 2, 3, 4, 6, 8, 9, 12, 18, 24, 36 and 72.
So the common factors of 54 and 72 are = 1, 2, 3, 6, 9 and 18.

**HOW ARE YOU GETTING ON?**

# THE REVISION SERIES

# ADDING AND SUBTRACTING

## ADDING AND SUBTRACTING

### HOW TO ADD

Once you understand the method of adding, these questions will become really easy!

The key to adding is positioning the digits so that they are in the correct column. The best way to demonstrate this is by example.

**Step 1** = write the biggest number first and then put the smallest number underneath.

**Step 2** = remember, the digits should be in the correct column:

**Step 3** = begin by adding the units column, and then the tens column i.e. from right to left.

**Step 4** = remember to carry over any numbers to the next column.

### _Example 1_

Work out 438 + 29

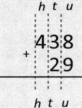

**Step 1** = line the numbers up starting from the right column.

**Step 2** = add the units column (8 + 9 = 17). The '1' needs to be carried over to the tens column.

**Step 3** = add the tens column (3 + 2 = 5). Remember to add the '1' that we carried over. (3 + 2 + 1 = 6).

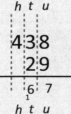

**Step 4** = there is no number to add the 4 to, so it would just be '4'.

## ADDING AND SUBTRACTING

# HOW TO SUBTRACT

The same method still applies when subtracting. You go about everything in the same way, but instead of adding the columns together, you subtract the numbers.

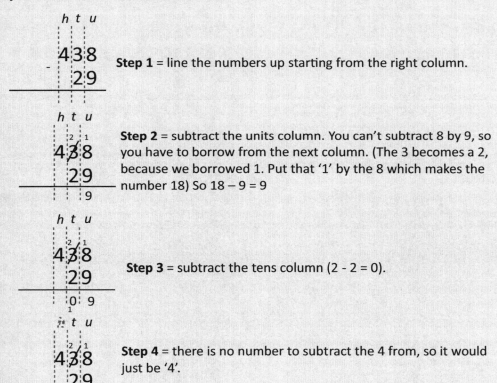

**Step 1** = line the numbers up starting from the right column.

**Step 2** = subtract the units column. You can't subtract 8 by 9, so you have to borrow from the next column. (The 3 becomes a 2, because we borrowed 1. Put that '1' by the 8 which makes the number 18) So 18 − 9 = 9

**Step 3** = subtract the tens column (2 - 2 = 0).

**Step 4** = there is no number to subtract the 4 from, so it would just be '4'.

---

Things to remember when adding or subtracting:

- Make sure you write the digits in the correct columns. Always write the numbers so that all of the numbers finish in the *units* column.
- If numbers are being carried over, remember to include these when adding up the column!
- If you are subtracting a small number by a big number, remember to BORROW from the NEXT column. Remember to cancel down the number from the column. (So if the number was 3 and you borrowed, this would then be a 2).
- If you have borrowed from a column, once the number is placed in the column you are working out, remember to read the number correctly. (If you borrowed 1 and put it with a 4, this would be 14).

**Question 1**

$$\begin{array}{r} 38 \\ + \quad 93 \\ \hline \\ \hline \end{array}$$

**Question 2**

$$\begin{array}{r} 124 \\ + \quad 32 \\ \hline \\ \hline \end{array}$$

**Question 3**

$$\begin{array}{r} 1294 \\ + \quad 732 \\ \hline \\ \hline \end{array}$$

**Question 4**

$$\begin{array}{r} 2195 \\ + \quad 243 \\ \hline \\ \hline \end{array}$$

**Question 5**

$$\begin{array}{r} 329 \\ - \quad 28 \\ \hline \\ \hline \end{array}$$

**Question 6**

$$\begin{array}{r} 48 \\ - \quad 39 \\ \hline \\ \hline \end{array}$$

**Question 7**

$$\begin{array}{r} 2395 \\ + \quad 3208 \\ \hline \\ \hline \end{array}$$

**Question 8**

$$\begin{array}{r} 10395 \\ + \quad 538 \\ \hline \\ \hline \end{array}$$

**Question 9**

$$\begin{array}{r} 4697 \\ - \quad 1564 \\ \hline \\ \hline \end{array}$$

**Question 10**

$$\begin{array}{r} 972 \\ - \quad 678 \\ \hline \\ \hline \end{array}$$

# ANSWERS TO ADDING AND SUBTRACTING

**Q1. 131**

EXPLANATION = 38 + 93 = 131

**Q2. 156**

EXPLANATION = 124 + 32 = 156

**Q3. 2,026**

EXPLANATION = 1,294 + 732 = 2,026

**Q4. 2,438**

EXPLANATION = 2,195 + 243 = 2,438

**Q5. 301**

EXPLANATION = 329 − 28 = 301

**Q6. 9**

EXPLANATION = 48 − 39 = 9

**Q7. 5,603**

EXPLANATION = 2,395 + 3,208 = 5,603

**Q8. 10,933**

EXPLANATION = 10,395 + 538 = 10,933

**Q9. 3,133**

EXPLANATION = 4,697 − 1,564 = 3,133

**Q10. 294**

EXPLANATION = 972 − 678 = 294

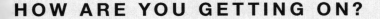 **HOW ARE YOU GETTING ON?**

THE
**REVISION**
SERIES

# MULTIPLYING AND DIVIDING

## MULTIPLYING AND DIVIDING

## HOW TO MULTIPLY

Multiply   =   Times

Sometimes you may be required to work out multiplications in your head. This is why it is a good idea to practice your times tables!

| 1 | 2 | 3 | 4 | 5 | 6 | 7 | 8 | 9 | 10 |
|---|---|---|---|---|---|---|---|---|---|
| 2 | 4 | 6 | 8 | 10 | 12 | 14 | 16 | 18 | 20 |
| 3 | 6 | 9 | 12 | 15 | 18 | 21 | 24 | 27 | 30 |
| 4 | 8 | 12 | 16 | 20 | 24 | 28 | 32 | 36 | 40 |
| 5 | 10 | 15 | 20 | 25 | 30 | 35 | 40 | 45 | 50 |
| 6 | 12 | 18 | 24 | 30 | 36 | 42 | 48 | 54 | 60 |
| 7 | 14 | 21 | 28 | 35 | 42 | 49 | 56 | 63 | 70 |
| 8 | 16 | 24 | 32 | 40 | 48 | 56 | 64 | 72 | 80 |
| 9 | 18 | 27 | 36 | 45 | 54 | 63 | 72 | 81 | 90 |
| 10 | 20 | 30 | 40 | 50 | 60 | 70 | 80 | 90 | 100 |

There are two methods you can use to work out multiplication sums. The first is the **grid method** and the other is the **vertical method.**

I am going to teach you both ways. Some people will find one method easier than the other. Unless the question specifically asks you otherwise, it does not matter which method you choose to use, so long as you reach the correct answer!

Let's take a look at the **grid method** first.

## MULTIPLYING AND DIVIDING

# THE GRID METHOD - MULTIPLICATION

Using the grid method requires you to break up the numbers using columns of units, tens, hundreds and so forth. The idea is, you break up the number and then multiply each part separately.

*Example 1*

456 x 17

**Step 1** = 400 (hundreds)
  50 (tens)
  6 (units)

**Step 2** = 10 (tens)
  7 (units)

| X | 400 | 50 | 6 |
|---|-----|----|----|
| 10 | | | |
| 7 | | | |

**Step 3** = multiply all of the columns by the rows.

| X | 400 | 50 | 6 |
|---|-----|----|----|
| 10 | 4,000 | 500 | 60 |
| 7 | 2,800 | 350 | 42 |

**Step 4** = working along each row, add up the totals

| X | 400 | 50 | 6 | Totals |
|---|-----|----|----|--------|
| 10 | 4,000 | 500 | 60 | 4,560 |
| 7 | 2,800 | 350 | 42 | 3,192 |

**Step 5** = 4,560 + 3,192 = **7,752**

Things to remember:

- Make sure you have broken the numbers up into the correct columns.
- Remember to add the rows up, and then calculate the overall total.
- You can also add up the total of each column, instead of adding up each row – you will still reach the correct answer!

## MULTIPLYING AND DIVIDING

## THE VERTICAL METHOD – MULTIPLICATION

When using the vertical method, the important thing to remember is to line up the columns in the correct order.

REMEMBER – units, tens, hundreds

*Example 1*

395 x 6

**Step 1** = begin by lining up the numbers in the correct columns.
**Step 2** = the small number (6) will be used to multiply each of the numbers of the larger number. (5 x 6)

```
  h  t  u
  3  9  5
        6
  ─────────
        0
       3
```

**Step 3** = now multiply the unit (6) by 9. (Remember to add the 3)

```
  h  t  u
  3  9  5
        6
  ─────────
     7  0
    5  3
```

**Step 4** = now multiply the unit (6) by 3. (Remember to add the 5)

```
  h  t  u
  3  9  5
        6
  ─────────
  2 3  7  0
    5  3
```

*Have you mastered this method?*

It does take a little while to get the hang of things, especially if you are working with larger numbers!

In the above example you were only working with one big number and one small number, but sometimes you might be asked to multiply two big numbers.

Again, the method is the same, but you break it down into two parts.

Let's have a look at a slightly harder question.

## MULTIPLYING AND DIVIDING

_Example 2_

214 x 44

**Step 1** = begin by lining up the numbers in the correct columns.
**Step 2** = multiply the top numbers by the unit (4) in the bottom number.

```
        h  t  u
        2  1  4
           4  4
        _____
        8  5  6
              1
```

**Step 3** = after you have multiplied the top numbers by the unit in the bottom number, multiply the top number by the number of tens in the bottom number (40).

_(40 x 4)_            _(40 x 10)_            _(40 x 200)_

```
  h  t  u            h  t  u            h  t  u
  2  1  4            2  1  4            2  1  4
     4  4               4  4               4  4
  _____         _____         _____
  8  5  6            8  5  6            8  5  6
        1                  1                  1
  1  6  0            1  6  0            1  6  0
  _____         _____         _____
                     4  0  0            4  0  0
                     _____         _____
                                        8  0  0  0
```

**Step 4** = add up all of the rows = 856 + 160 + 400 + 8,000 = **9,416**

REMEMBER = if you are multiplying a decimal, the best way to answer this is to ignore the decimal point, do the sum, and then add it back into the answer at the end. (The decimal point would be added the same amount of places as it was in the question i.e. if two numbers come after the decimal point in the question, then two numbers would need to come after the decimal point in the answer).

## MULTIPLYING AND DIVIDING

### DIVIDING NUMBERS

Now that you have mastered multiplication, let's learn the method for dividing numbers.

Questions relating to division could use the following words:

- "Divided by";
- "Shared by";
- "Into".

This is the **symbol** for division

$$28 \div 4$$

$$4 \overline{)28} \quad \boxed{7}$$

The **answer** is written on top.

The large number goes **inside** the brackets.

This is basically asking *'how many times does 4 go into 28'*.

The answer to this would be 7.
(4 goes into 28 seven times).

**REMEMBER** = if you are dividing a decimal, the best way to answer this is to ignore the decimal point, do the sum, and t hen add it back into the answer at the end. (The decimal point would be added the same amount of places as it was in the question i.e. if two numbers come after the decimal point in the question, then two numbers would need to come after the decimal point in the answer).

### A DIVISION SUM CAN BE WRITTEN IN MANY DIFFERENT WAYS

$$56 \div 8$$    is the same as....    $$8 \overline{)56}$$    is the same as....    $$\frac{56}{8}$$

### THE REMAINDER...

Sometimes, you may be given a division sum whereby the number does not go EXACTLY into it. This is called the **remainder**. This simply means 'the part left over'.

For example, 45 ÷ 6 = goes 7 times, but there are 5 left over.

So, this would be written as <u>7 remainder 5</u> or <u>7 r 5</u>.

## MULTIPLYING AND DIVIDING

There are two methods to dividing numbers. These are **short division** and **long division**. The method that you will need to use, depends on how big the number is.

## SHORT DIVISION – DIVIDING

*Example 1*

What is 504 ÷ 9?

**Step 1** = begin by laying out the question as shown:

$$9 \overline{\smash{)}504}$$

**Step 2** = how many times does 9 go into 5 = 0. Because the 5 doesn't go into 9, you need to move the 5 just above the 0 to make (50).

$$9 \overline{\smash{)}5^{5}04}$$

**Step 3** = how many times does 9 into 50 = 5 (put this on top of the line above the (50). It has a remainder of 5 (put this next to the 4 to make (54)).

$$9 \overline{\smash{)}5\,^{5}0^{5}4}$$
(answer: 5)

**Step 4** = how many times does 9 into 54 = 6. Put the 6 on top of the line next to the 5.

$$9 \overline{\smash{)}5\,^{5}0^{5}4}$$
(answer: 56)

**Step 5** = so the correct answer is 56.

*Example 2*

What is 940 ÷ 8?

**Step 1** = how many times does 8 go into 9 = 1. (With a remainder of 1).

$$8 \overline{\smash{)}940}$$

**Step 2** = how many times does 8 go into 14 = 1. (With a remainder of 6).

$$8 \overline{\smash{)}9^{1}40}$$
(answer: 1)

**Step 4** = how many times does 8 go into 60 = 7. (With a remainder of 5).

$$8 \overline{\smash{)}9^{1}4^{6}0}$$
(answer: 117 r 5)

**Step 5** = because there are no more numbers to divide by, we have finished the sum. There is still a remainder of 5. So 940 divided by 8 is **117 remainder 5 (117 r 5).**

## MULTIPLYING AND DIVIDING

## LONG DIVISION – DIVIDING

*Example 1*

What is 2,640 ÷ 20

**Step 1** = how many times does 20 go into 2 = 0.

```
        0
     _____
20 ) 2 6 4 0
```

**Step 2** = how many times does 20 go into 26 = 1 (Remainder of 6). Underneath the 26, write the whole number that goes into 26 (20). Subtract this from the 26 to find the remainder (6).

```
        0 1
     _____
          2
20 ) 2 6 4 0
   -  2 0  ↓
     _____
        6 4
```

**Step 3** = now you are working with 64. How many times does 20 go into 64 = 3 (Remainder of 4). Underneath the 64, write the whole number that goes into 64 (60) and subtract that by the 64.

```
        0 1 3
     _____
          2
20 ) 2 6 4 0
   -  2 0  ↓
     _____
    -   6 4
        6 0
     _____
          4
```

**Step 4** = Now you are working with 40. How many times does 20 go into 40 = 2. Underneath the 40, write the whole number that goes into 40 (40), and subtract the two numbers. This gives you 0, which means the sum is complete.

**Step 5** = 2,640 ÷ 20 = **132**

```
        0 1 3 2
     _____
          2
20 ) 2 6 4 0
   -  2 0  ↓ |
     _____
    -   6 4  |
        6 0  ↓
     _____
          4 0
          4 0
     _____
          0 0
```

## Question 1

a) 458 x 10

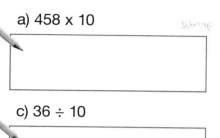

b) 36.98 x 100

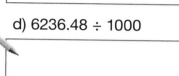

c) 36 ÷ 10

d) 6236.48 ÷ 1000

## Question 2

Using short division, work out 7068 ÷ 38.

## Question 3

Fill in the missing blanks.

a) 1000 x [    ] = 3125

b) [    ] x 100 = 3.216

c) 32.568 ÷ [    ] = 3.2568

d) [    ] ÷ 100 = 9.6312

## Question 4

Fill in the missing blanks of the multiplication grid.

| X | 300 | | 2 |
|---|---|---|---|
| 20 | 6,000 | 1,400 | |
| 5 | | 350 | |

**Question 5**

$$15 \overline{)4\ 2\ 9\ 6}$$

**Question 6**

$$7 \overline{)9\ 4\ 9\ 9}$$

**Question 7**

$$21 \overline{)9\ 5\ 9\ 7}$$

**Question 8**

$$16 \overline{)1\ 8\ 9\ 9\ 2}$$

**Question 9**

$$
\begin{array}{r}
5\ 3\ 6 \\
\times \qquad 8 \\
\hline
\\
\hline
\end{array}
$$

**Question 10**

$$
\begin{array}{r}
1\ 4\ 6\ 8 \\
\times \qquad 4 \\
\hline
\\
\hline
\end{array}
$$

**Question 11**

$$
\begin{array}{r}
3\ 9\ 8 \\
\times \qquad 5 \\
\hline
\\
\hline
\end{array}
$$

**Question 12**

$$
\begin{array}{r}
1\ 2\ 3\ 4 \\
\times \qquad 6 \\
\hline
\\
\hline
\end{array}
$$

## Question 13

Lola spends £1,456.80 in 20 days. How much does Lola spend per day?

## Question 14

Using the grid method, work out 2,324 x 15

## Question 15

Using long division, work out 3204 ÷ 18

## Question 16

a) Tammy has 6 cats. She needs 2 tins of food per cat, per day. Each can of food costs £0.89. How much does Tammy spend in 5 days?

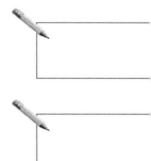

b) Joe, Ryan and Harrison share a bag of sweets. The bag contains 135 sweets. How many sweets does each person get?

# ANSWERS TO MULTIPLYING AND DIVIDING

**Q1. a) 4580**

   **b) 3,698**

   **c) 3.6**

   **d) 6.23648**

**Q2. 186**

$$
\begin{array}{r}
0\ 0\ 1\ 8\ 6 \\
\hline
38\,)\ 7\ 0^{70}\ 6^{22}\ 8
\end{array}
$$

**Q3. a) 3.125**

EXPLANATION = 3125 ÷ 1000 = 3.125 (1000 x 3.125 = 3125).

   **b) 0.03216**

EXPLANATION = 3.216 ÷ 100 = 0.03216 (0.03216 x 100 = 3.216).

   **c) 10**

EXPLANATION = 32.568 ÷ 10 = 3.2568

   **d) 963.12**

EXPLANATION = 9.6312 x 100 = 963.12 (963.12 ÷ 100 = 9.6312).

**Q4. Your answer should look like this:**

| X | 300 | 70 | 2 |
|---|---|---|---|
| 20 | 6,000 | 1,400 | 40 |
| 5 | 1,500 | 350 | 10 |

**Q5. 286 r 6**

```
        0  2  8  6  r 6
      4  12    9
15 ) 4  2  9  6
```

**Q6. 1,357**

```
      1  3  5  7
         2   3   4
 7 ) 9  4  9  9
```

**Q7. 457**

```
        0  4  5  7
         9  11  14
21 ) 9  5  9  7
```

**Q8. 1,187**

```
       0  1  1  8  7
         1   2  29  11
16 ) 1  8  9  9  2
```

**Q9. 4,288**

```
      5  3  6
 x          8
  ─────────────
  4  2  8  8
   4    2    4
```

**Q10. 5,872**

```
   1  4  6  8
 x          4
  ─────────────
  5  8  7  2
   1    2    3
```

**11. 1,990**

```
    3 9 8
          5
  1 9 9 0
    4   4
```

**12. 7,404**

```
  1 2 3 4
          6
  7 4 0 4
  1   2   2
```

**13. £72.84**

XPLANATION = £1,456.80 ÷ 20 days = £72.84

**14. 34,860**

| X | 2000 | 300 | 20 | 4 | TOTALS |
|---|------|-----|-----|---|--------|
| 10 | 20000 | 3000 | 200 | 40 | 23240 |
| 5 | 10000 | 1500 | 100 | 20 | 11620 |
| | | | | | 34860 |

**15. 178**

```
      0 0 1 7 8
           3 2
  8 ) 3 2 0 4
     - 3 0 6 ↓
         1 4 4
       -
         1 4 4
           0 0
```

**Q16. a) £53.40**

EXPLANATION = 0.89 x 2 (tins per cat) = £1.78. £1.78 x 6 (cats) = £10.68.
£10.68 x 5 (days) = £53.40

**b) 45**

EXPLANATION = 135 ÷ 3 = 45

THE
**REVISION**
SERIES

# WORKING WITH MONEY

## WORKING WITH MONEY

Money problems are fairly easy to work out if you have mastered calculating numbers via adding, subtracting, multiplying and dividing.

The main difference between calculating whole numbers, and calculating money, is that money sums usually have a decimal point. As long as you know how to line up the decimal points in the correct column, this will be really easy!

*Example 1*

What is £3.20 + £8.75?

**Step 1** = write out the numbers, with the numbers in the correct headings.

$$
\begin{array}{r}
£3.20 \\
+\ £8.75 \\
\hline
\end{array}
$$

**Step 2** = you have already learned how to add numbers, so use the same method. Just remember to add in the decimal point and the £ sign.

$$
\begin{array}{r}
£3.20 \\
+\ £8.75 \\
\hline
£11.95
\end{array}
$$

*Example 2*

What is £5.71 – 98p?

**Step 1** = write out the numbers, with the numbers in the correct headings.
   remember, 98p has 0 pounds, therefore this should be written as £0.98

$$
\begin{array}{r}
£5.71 \\
-\ £0.98 \\
\hline
\end{array}
$$

**Step 2** = you have already learned how to subtract numbers, so use the same method. Just remember to add in the decimal point and the £ sign.

$$
\begin{array}{r}
£5.71 \\
-\ £0.98 \\
\hline
£4.73
\end{array}
$$

You will most likely be given questions that are money problems. For example, if a tin of dog food costs £0.67p, and you need to buy 5 tins, you would need to multiply 67p by 5.

0.67 x 5 = £3.35

## Question 1

Work out the following sums.

a)
$$£ \ 6.85$$
$$+$$
$$£ \ 4.68$$
_____

b)
$$£ \ 13.24$$
$$+$$
$$£ \ 25.63$$
_____

c)
$$£ \ 10.08$$
$$-$$
$$£ \ \ 5.73$$
_____

d)
$$£ \ 182.54$$
$$-$$
$$£ \ 112.35$$
_____

## Question 2

A primary school is going on a school trip. In total, there are 48 pupils attending the trip. Each pupil has to pay £23.80 to attend. How much is this in total?

## Question 3

A family of four spend £368.80 on their weekly food shopping. If the four members of the family split the cost equally, how much will each of them pay?

## Question 4

Anil goes in to a shop. He is debating which pack of drinks is the best dea
Read the sale sign for the drinks, and work out whether the 6-pack or th
8-pack is the best value for money.

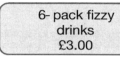

| 6- pack fizzy | 8- pack fizzy |
| drinks | drinks |
| £3.00 | £4.80 |

## Question 5

Jason goes to the cinema with his friend Matt. Each of them buys a tub o
popcorn. For 800 grams of popcorn, it costs £2.20. How much would eac
200 grams of popcorn cost?

## Question 6

Work out the following sums.

a)     £  236.98
   -
       £  105.69
   _____

   _____

b)     £  789.42
   +
       £  245.53
   _____

   _____

c)     £  86.23
   +
       £     9.76
   _____

   _____

d)     £  468.74
   +
       £     57.42
   _____

   _____

# ANSWERS TO WORKING WITH MONEY

**Q1. a) £11.53**

    **b) £38.87**

    **c) £4.35**

    **d) £70.19**

**Q2. £1,142.40**

EXPLANATION = 48 x £23.80 = £1,142.40

**Q3. £92.20**

EXPLANATION = £368.80 ÷ 4 = £92.20

**Q4. 6-pack deal**

EXPLANATION = 6-pack (£3.00 ÷ 6 = 0.50p per can).

8-pack (£4.80 ÷ 8 = 0.60p per can). Therefore the best deal is the 6-pack deal.

**Q5. £0.55p**

EXPLANATION = if 800 grams of popcorn is £2.20. That means 200 grams is 4 times less. So £2.20 ÷ 4 = £0.55p

**Q6. a) £131.29**

    **b) £1034.95**

    **c) £95.99**

    **d) £526.16**

**HOW ARE YOU GETTING ON?**

THE
**REVISION**
SERIES

# ORDER
# OF
# OPERATIONS

## ORDER OF OPERATIONS

# B I D M A S

Some sums may require you to carry out more than one operation. For example, you might be asked to add two numbers, then subtract it by another number, and multiply it by another number.

### REMEMBER = BIDMAS

(**B**rackets), (**I**ndices), (**D**ivision), (**M**ultiplication), (**A**ddition), (**S**ubtraction)

There is a set method in Maths that you should ALWAYS use when working out multiple operations.

<u>In order, you should first work out:</u>

- **Brackets** – (5 + 6);
- **Indices** – i.e. powers ($2^2$ or $3^3$);
- **Divisions** and **Multiplications** (in the order that you find them);
- **Additions** and **Subtractions** (in the order that you find them).

If you don't follow the rules of BIDMAS, you could end up with multiple possible answers. Only one answer would be correct, and it will depend on working out the operations in the correct order.

*Example*

Work out the following sum.

$$6 + 4 \times 5$$

**Step 1** = using BIDMAS, work out which operations you will be working with (in the question above you have an addition and a multiplication).
**Step 2** = you should know that multiplication comes before addition, so work out the multiplication part of the sum first!
**Step 3** = the multiplication part = $4 \times 5 = 20$
**Step 4** = now finish with the addition part = $20 + 6 = 26$.
**Step 5** = so the correct answer for the above question is **26**.

*Can you see, if we did the addition part first (6 + 4 = 10), and then did the multiplication (10 x 5 = 50), we would have a different answer. This would be incorrect! Remember, multiplication comes before addition!*

# B I D M A S

**Question 1**

$(4 + 3) \times (6 - 2)$

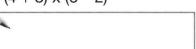

**Question 2**

$4 \div 2 \times 9$

**Question 3**

$4 \times (6 + 5)$

**Question 4**

$6 + 3 \times 7$

**Question 5**

$3 + 8 \div 2$

**Question 6**

$3 \times 6 - 5 \times 2$

**Question 7**

$5 + (9 - 4) \times 3$

**Question 8**

$8 + (4 \times 2^2) - 5$

**Question 9**

$7 \times 2 \times 5$

**Question 10**

$3 \times (20 \div 4)$

**Question 11**

$2 \times 6 \div 2$

**Question 12**

$2 \times 4^2 - 6$

# ANSWERS TO ORDERS OF OPERATIONS

**Q1. 28**

EXPLANATION = brackets first (4 + 3 = 7), (6 − 2 = 4).
Then the multiplication = 7 x 4 = 28

**Q2. 18**

EXPLANATION = divide first = 4 ÷ 2 = 2. Then the multiplication = 2 x 9 = 1

**Q3. 44**

EXPLANATION = brackets first = (6 + 5 = 11). Then the multiplication = 11 x
4 = 44

**Q4. 27**

EXPLANATION = multiplication first = 3 x 7 = 21. Then the addition = 21 + 6
= 27

**Q5. 7**

EXPLANATION = division first = 8 ÷ 2 = 4. Then the addition = 4 + 3 = 7

**Q6. 8**

EXPLANATION = multiplications first = 3 x 6 = 18. Then the other
multiplication = 5 x 2 = 10. Then the subtraction = 18 − 10 = 8

**Q7. 20**

EXPLANATION = brackets first = (9 − 4 = 5). Then the multiplication = 15.
Then the addition = 15 + 5 = 20

**Q8. 19**

EXPLANATION = brackets first ($2^2$ = 2 x 2 = 4. 4 x 4 = 16). Then the addition
= 16 + 8 = 24. Then the subtraction = 24 − 5 = 19

**Q9. 70**

EXPLANATION = multiplication first = 2 x 5 = 10. Then the multiplication =
10 x 7 = 70

**Q10. 15**

EXPLANATION = brackets first (20 ÷ 4 = 5). Then the multiplication = 5 x 3 = 15

**Q11. 6**

EXPLANATION = division first = 6 ÷ 2 = 3. Then the multiplication = 3 x 2 = 6

**Q12. 26**

EXPLANATION = indices first = $4^2$ = 4 x 4 = 16. Then the multiplication = 16 x 2 = 32. Then the subtraction = 32 – 6 = 26

**HOW ARE YOU GETTING ON?**

# So... how did you get on?

*Using the 'how did you get on' boxes at the end of each section, tally up how many thumbs up, thumbs down, and okay thumbs you scored, and see what you scored most!*

*Don't forget, to get more FREE questions visit:*
**www.PsychometricTestsOnline.co.uk**

*Good luck with your Maths tests!*

Anil